AMERICA

A PHOTOGRAPHIC HISTORY

This book is dedicated to the memory of Ronan Andersen (1919-1989).

Text
James Summerville

Photographs
National Archives, Washington, DC
UPI/Bettmann

Design
Hans Verkroost

Commissioning Editor
Andrew Preston

Publishing Assistant
Edward Doling

Picture Research
Kenneth Johnston
Leora Kahn

Editorial
David Gibbon
Fleur Robertson

Production
Ruth Arthur
David Proffit
Sally Connolly

Director of Production
Gerald Hughes

Director of Publishing
David Gibbon

MALLARD PRESS

An imprint of BDD Promotional Books Company, Inc,
666 Fifth Avenue, New York, NY 10103.

Mallard Press and its accompanying design and logo
are trademarks of BDD Promotional Book Company, Inc.

CLB 2349
© 1990 Archive Publishing, a division of Colour Library Books Ltd,
Godalming, Surrey, England.
First published in the United States of America
in 1990 by The Mallard Press.
Printed and bound in Italy by New Interlitho.
All rights reserved.
ISBN 0 792 45380 8

A M E R I C A

A PHOTOGRAPHIC HISTORY

JAMES SUMMERVILLE

MALLARD PRESS

Americans made themselves, not their awesomely rich and spacious land, the subjects of their earliest camera work. Robert Cornelius made the first photograph of a human being, in November 1839, by leaping in front of a daguerreotype camera in the yard of his Philadelphia home. In the years that followed, itinerant photographers roamed the countryside in wagons or sailed the rivers on flatboats outfitted with a studio. Anyone with the patience to sit for the long exposure that the primitive box required – and of course with the money to pay the hefty sum charged – could have a "portrait," which was a kind of stay against death and loss. Bereft parents commissioned pictures of children in their coffins. Men anxious to strike it rich in the California gold rush anxiously sat for a photograph that they could leave behind.

So indifferent to history, Americans in time became passionate to preserve the present moment on film, and the camera would eventually become a means for understanding the past. Millions have watched the film of President John Kennedy as he was struck in the head by rifle fire. The photo of astronaut Buzz Aldrin saluting the flag at Tranquility Base, on the moon, became an icon of American technological achievement. Row after row of one week's casualties in Vietnam, published in *Life* magazine, brought that war home and public opposition to a new intensity.

As a people, we have a touching, naive faith in the truth of a picture and, indeed, its superiority to its subject. What bride and groom in modern America hasn't been harried into a blissful pose, assured that their memories would be more perfect than the anxious day? How many fans have encountered their movie idol, only to find that "he doesn't look a thing like his pictures"?

Providence seemed to have great things in store for the young nation, and the camera would possess it all. When President James K. Polk added Oregon to the Union, Great Britain objected to his boundary claims with its possession of Canada. Pictures of the disputed land were added to the legal documents. As immigrants headed west during the 1840s toward the new states of California and Texas they hung camera portraits of the great and famous on the walls of the saloons in their clapboard towns. Not coincidentally, the oldest pictures of the White House and the Capitol date from Polk's years. The engraving of Henry Clay's famous farewell address to the U.S. Senate, in 1842, was based on actual photographs of members of Congress who heard it. Mathew Brady sent a disciple to Nashville so that Andrew Jackson, the hero of New Orleans, might sit for posterity during

his last days. In 1844 Brady opened his first photographic gallery. This American photographic pioneer had a sense of mission toward the nation's past, brief though it was by comparison to the nation of the Old World. "From the first," he wrote, "I regarded myself as under obligation to my country to preserve the faces of its historic men and mothers."

Surely a Divine Providence so profligate in His blessings on this land meant for all Americans to enjoy them. So reasoned the social reformers of these years. Some tried to persuade men to cherish the Gospel and swear off the bottle. Others founded schools for the young. At the American Women's Rights Convention in 1848, Elizabeth Cady Stanton and Lucretia Mott called for giving women the right to vote. It would take seventy years – and photographs of suffragists being hoisted into paddy wagons – to achieve their goal. Later generations of crusaders would employ the camera to document conditions in slums, asylums, factories.

Two women sewing in their kitchen in a slum. Often this kind of labor was the only sort available for women with young children.

The cause of abolition won the most ardent and vociferous souls, and they helped bring on Civil War. By the late 1840s, revolution and famine in Europe had swelled migration. The war with Mexico opened vast territory – and the question of whether it would be slave or free.

The Compromise of 1850 admitted California as a free state and organized territories out of the other lands without restrictions as to slavery. But another provision of the Compromise, a stringent law requiring return of fleeing slaves to their owners, aroused bitter hatred among many in the north. Those who wanted to free the slaves still depended on word-pictures; few photographers seem to have penetrated the plantation South. A devastating portrayal of slave life, Harriet Beecher Stowe's *Uncle Tom's Cabin ; Or Life Among the Lowly* sold ten thousand copies a week when it appeared in 1852 (in England, a total of one and a half million copies was sold).

When Congress decided in 1854 to allow the settlers of the Kansas and Nebraska territories to decide whether or not they would accept slaves, pro-slavery and abolitionist men rushed there to establish a majority. In Kansas the two sides set up rival governments and came to pitched battle. Both the dominant political parties, the Democrats and the Whigs, had called for acceptance of the Compromise of 1850 and an end to agitation over the slavery question. But a new party, the Republicans, comprising mainly abolitionists, demanded repeal of the anti-slavery act and repeal of the hated fugitive slave law.

The presidential election of 1856 was fought out along the lines of north versus South, slavery versus anti-slavery. The victorious Democrat, James Buchanan, declared he would not interfere with slavery in the states where it existed and supported popular sovereignty in the territories. Few were placated by his moderate position.

More talk of disunion arose – in the north and in the south – when the Supreme Court handed down the Dred Scott decision in 1857. Scott, a slave, had not been freed just because his owner took him into free territory, the court held. The clear implication was that Congress had no right to deprive an owner of property rights in slaves, anywhere. Along with the trouble in Kansas, the new Republican Party was suddenly handed a powerful campaign issue. Meanwhile, Southerners understood northern support for John Brown's attempt to foment a slave insurrection as a call for an end to slavery at any price.

As Abraham Lincoln of Illinois was striding toward the Republican nomination in 1860, Queen Victoria ordered *cartes de visite*, or "visiting cards," taken of herself and the royal family. In the United States Mathew Brady reproduced a photograph of Lincoln in the *carte de visite* style. More than one hundred thousand copies of his picture circulated all over the country.

Lincoln's moderate view – that he would not interfere with slavery where it existed but was opposed to extending it to the territories – was unacceptable to Southern Democrats. When their party rejected a pro-slavery platform, they bolted. Arriving back home, they announced they would lead their states out of the Union if Lincoln became President. On November 6, 1861, he won the election by a minority of the popular vote but a solid majority in the electoral college.

Home of the most militant pro-slavery politicians, South Carolina seceded on December 20, followed before summer by eleven other states. Lincoln called for volunteers to put down the "insurrection." He refused yet to call it war, but war it now was, as he well knew. In June Tennessee became the final state to join the Confederacy.

Although technical improvements had decreased exposure times, the camera still could capture movement only rarely. Thus, out of the thousands of Civil War photographs, only four show men in combat. But photography played an important part in the war. Hand-drawn maps could be reproduced and circulated to field commanders. And the camp follower was everywhere, with his cumbersome equipment and colorful tent, making portraits for family and friends back home.

The life of the common soldier was brutal, nothing like the romanticized accounts that many veterans recalled many years later. Both Union and Confederate forces experienced chronic shortages of clothing and shoes, while Southern armies lived on the edge of starvation. And the camera showed the dead, for the first time in a major conflict. As a reporter for the *New York Times* noted, "If [Brady] has not brought bodies home and laid them on our doorstep, he has done something like that."

The first year of the fight produced an awful toll of dead: Union General Ulysses S. Grant broke through the Southern strongholds of the Mississippi Valley in the winter of 1862. Then, in April, he suffered thirteen thousand casualties at Shiloh, and his Confederate opposite sustained eleven thousand killed or wounded. The South won an important victory at Manassas, Virginia, in August, and Robert E. Lee, commanding the Army of Northern Virginia, prepared to invade the north. But on September 17, there occurred the Battle of Antietam, the bloodiest day of the war, with ten thousand casualties on either side. Brady photographed Lincoln on the battlefield, his great angular frame standing a head taller than any of his commanders, and the famous stovepipe hat reaching for the treetops.

It was 1863 that proved the year of decision. Grant lay siege to Vicksburg, on the Mississippi River, and when he won, the Union had split the Confederacy north to south. In the east, Chancellorsville became a great Southern victory, but clouded by the loss of one of the Confederacy's most brilliant tacticians, Thomas "Stonewall" Jackson.

From July 1-3, the decisive battle took place at Gettysburg, in Pennsylvania. Lee and James Longstreet directed their forces against entrenched Union positions, and were thrown back by superior numbers. From then on, the South lacked enough men to mount an offensive into enemy territory.

After the fall of Vicksburg, the day after Gettysburg, the outcome of the war seems clear in retrospect. Perhaps it did to Lincoln as well. Dedicating the Gettysburg battlefield in November with one of the most famous orations of all time, he referred to the honored dead of both sides and predicted "a new birth of freedom, that government of the people, by the people, and for the people shall not perish from the earth." A few weeks later, he offered a pardon to all Confederates who would simply take a loyalty oath.

But some of the bloodiest fighting and most senseless deaths followed. In June 1864, Grant and General George Meade led a hundred thousand men against Lee's army, entrenched around the Confederate capital of Richmond. At the battle of the Wilderness, then at Spotsylvania, then at Cold Harbor, both sides struggled in useless, inconclusive slaughter. One Confederate general remarked, "This is not war, it's murder." Grant lost sixty thousand men, equal to the South's entire strength. Between twenty-five and thirty thousand Confederates fell, but given the declining manpower resources of the South, this was a far more devastating figure than the North's. Grant proceeded to lay siege to Petersburg, the "back door" to Richmond.

The Confederates made one last desperate and noble dash toward Washington, and actually entered the District of Columbia only to turn back when Union reinforcements arrived. In the western theatre, the reckless John Bell Hood took command of Union forces. But it was William Tecumseh Sherman who scored the blow that convinced many Southerners they could not win. He captured Atlanta in September and burned much of the city to the ground. That fall, he marched his troops to the sea, laying the countryside waste, then turned north through the Carolinas, leaving more devastation in his path. When Hood tried one last vainglorious assault on the Union stronghold of Nashville, his army was virtually destroyed.

President Davis named Robert E. Lee commander-in-chief of the Confederacy that winter, but Lee knew the cause was hopeless. Lincoln, hoping to spare needless deaths, offered the South generous terms for surrender. But when the Confederates were forced out of Richmond on April 2, the President went there and sat down in Davis's chair, a boyish grin on his homely face.

A week later, April 8, 1865, General Lee offered his sword to General Grant at Appomatox Courthouse, Virginia. Grant refused it, and told Lee that the officers and men were free to go home, with their own horses. After surrendering all other equipment, the officers were also allowed to keep their sidearms.

Lincoln wanted a reconstruction of the nation based on such generous conciliation. He did not live to preside over it. On April 14, John Wilkes Booth, an actor with Southern sympathies, shot the President to death as he was attending a play in Washington.

It is idle to speculate whether Lincoln could have reconstructed the nation "with charity for all." But historians generally agree that he was succeeded in office by men of lesser stature, ability, and vision. Andrew Johnson, sworn in three hours after Lincoln expired, proposed that each Southern state could rejoin the Union once ten percent of its population had taken a loyalty oath and after a convention had repudiated secession, ratified the Thirteenth Amendment abolishing slavery, and met other relatively mild conditions. But a majority of Republicans in Congress determined to impose harsher terms, including black male suffrage. These radicals demanded that the military governments in the conquered South report directly to Congress. Johnson fired his Secretary of War, and the president otherwise resisted the legislature's attempt to direct reconstruction. In the winter of 1868, the House impeached him (the equivalent of a grand jury indictment) for violating a law requiring that Congress concur in the firing of executive officers where the Constitution requires its consent to appoint them. The Senate sat as the trial court, and by a single vote found him not guilty. Nonetheless, Johnson left the White House discredited.

Federal troops remained in the South under his successor, the Union hero, Ulysses S. Grant. Under the army's eye, blacks, and whites without property, voted and held office for the first time in Southern history. Missionaries from congregations in the north opened schools for blacks, and many of these schools grew into colleges and universities. The old aristocratic families accepted Congress's terms and bided their time as Southern states rejoined the Union – and their leaders dismantled Reconstruction. By 1880 the ideology of white supremacy dominated the region. In the next twenty years segregation became codified in the "Jim Crow" laws (requiring separation of races on street cars and in other public facilities) and in various statutes that restricted black voting. With labor of black sharecropping – a penurious condition only a step above slavery – the South was producing more cotton than it did before the devastating war.

The north had won in part because of its technological superiority. The railroads were laid westward, opening new markets for beef and bread to farmers and cattlemen. America was hurtling toward industrial might, as finance capitalism replaced a subsistence economy, and invention brought forward new technologies and made older ones available to the masses. The camera, for example, followed the rail lines across the Great Plains, recording the ceremonies that marked completion of new links, vistas of the Rockies, Yellowstone, the Grand Canyon, and Yosemite. The Eastman Kodak company placed a hand-held box camera on the market in 1889. Suddenly, anyone patient enough to master the intricate operation could take pictures. By 1900 there were one hundred thousand of these cameras in the hands of amateurs, as compared to eight thousand horseless carriages.

Fittingly, the first photograph to appear in a newspaper was of a shantytown, at least as much a symbol of the new economic order as the gleaming iron rail or the dynamo. Growth and prosperity were vastly uneven across the industrial belt rising from Pittsburgh to Chicago. Machines and mines needed cheap labor, and millions came to the United States from Europe to supply it. In the South, poor blacks and, in the north, poor whites sustained the economy, the latter building modern industrial

America. But for twenty years after the panic of 1873, the nation was roiled by disputes between workers and owners of the textile factories, coal mines, steel plants. A photographer captured the strike of Baltimore and Ohio Railroad workers in 1877. In 1890 Jacob Riis, America's first noted photojournalist, published *How the Other Half Lives*, a book depicting slum conditions based on photographs. Others with a conscience and a camera recorded a ten-year old boy sewing in a New York sweatshop, and children working in coal mines.

A foreigner arriving in New York to seek work would often be met by a precinct captain from Tammany Hall, the Democratic organization, who would offer him a tenement room and a job in exchange for his vote. The Democrats tried to parlay the power and influence of such big city machines into an effective coalition with the resurgent Southern aristocrats. But on a national basis, they only stalemated the Republicans, who enjoyed the backing of Morgan, steel magnate Andrew Carnegie, and oil baron John D. Rockefeller. With unstinting financial help from this ilk, the Republicans elected a series of nonentities as president for most of the 1880s and 1890s – and achieved the dominance of *laissez-faire* capitalism. The national government proved ineffective in addressing the issues of economic dislocation.

As hard times continued among farmers and strikes proved more violent and disruptive, the political and economic order groaned under the stresses of dissatisfaction. In the south and west disgruntled farmers banded together in groups like the Grange and the Southern Alliance to seek state regulation of railroad rates and cooperate in measures that would assist farm families to get out of debt. In 1890 a number of these farmers' interest groups, as well as representatives from industrial labor, met at Topeka, Kansas, to form the Populist Party. By 1892 the organization held one governorship, four state legislatures, and fielded a presidential candidate. When a severe depression struck the nation the following year, President Grover Cleveland stood disgraced and the Populists' ambitions – and their numbers – swelled.

In 1896, however, the Democrats nominated for President a Populist hero, 36-year-old William Jennings Bryan. A powerful orator, the former Nebraska congressman called for a ten-hour work day and government regulation of the railroads and utilities. Bryan's chief plank was "free silver". Backers of this chimerical notion blamed the nation's economic woes on the requirement that every dollar had to be backed by its value in gold. Bryan's "silver tongue" argued that using the more plentiful precious metal, silver, could increase the money in circulation, putting more dollars in everybody's pocket.

As he crisscrossed the country, Bryan inspired many with his magnetism, but his rhetoric frightened the giant capitalists. The railroad plutocrats, steel company magnates and oil barons spent lavish sums in behalf of the Republican nominee William McKinley; some seven million dollars compared to three hundred thousand spent by the Democrats. On election day it paid off, with a decisive McKinley victory. Nearly forty years after it first won the White House, the party found the electoral base that would keep it the majority party until the New Deal: middle-class townspeople who rallied around its call for "sound money," the protective tariff, and nationalism in foreign policy. Bryan sought the new immigrants; McKinley's followers, by and large, would have shunned them if they had actually met any. Yet the reform spirit had not been broken. Over the next forty years, many of the populists' ideas would become law.

Not long after his reelection in 1900, President McKinley was shot to death by an anarchist, and the vice president, Theodore Roosevelt, succeeded him. Assistant secretary of the navy when the U.S. declared war on Spain in 1898, Roosevelt had resigned and received a commission to go to fight in Cuba. A genuinely fearless man, Roosevelt was also a relentless self-promoter, and he turned his war exploits into a press hungry for America's triumph in this "splendid little war." The coverage made Roosevelt governor of New York, and the war, though it lasted only six weeks, made the United States an imperial power, bringing under its flag the Philippines, Guam, Puerto Rico, Hawaii, and Cuba as a protectorate.

A gifted natural athlete and man of exceptional stamina, Roosevelt personified the strenuous life and martial spirit of the new America built on steel and empire. If, like Bryan's, his speech occasionally exceeded his grasp, Roosevelt as President nonetheless worked to redress some of the worst abuses of industrial capitalism. His administration gave to a federal commission the power to regulate freight rates, regulation over railroad rates, and enactment of a pure food and drug law. In foreign affairs, he completed the nation's turn from its post-Civil War isolationism. His most dramatic and controversial achievement was the acquisition of the Panamanian isthmus, permitting the United States to build an interoceanic canal.

With its new technological prowess, and flush with the triumph of business conservatism and military might, the United States stood tall as the new century began. The nation was prosperous, too, but not all shared in that. The farmers, who had nearly fomented a revolution, still eked out a living between spring planting and fall harvest. As for the great industrial machine, it depended upon factory hands who spent long hours for low pay over dangerous, dirty looms, lathes, or presses.

The voices of dissatisfaction and dissent did not cease. The growing cities gave rise to a whole new arena for reformers. Case workers, public health nurses, and "good government" men attacked overcrowding, poor sanitation, crime, and the private ownership of essential monopolies like electric services and streetcars. These "Progressives," were in some respects heirs of the Populists. Both groups believed that the large concentrations of economic power – from big oil concerns to the local utilities – posed a threat to political democracy. The Progressives argued that, through one means or another, government had to control these combinations. On the other side of the controversy, the representatives of big business replied that market forces would provide the answer while government interference would only make the problem worse.

At the national level, Progressives won important triumphs. The Seventeenth Amendment to the Constitution, ratified in 1913, provided for the election of United States Senators directly by vote of the people, putting an end to the notoriously corrupt process of election by the state legislatures. The Eighteenth Amendment prohibited the manufacture and sale of alcoholic beverages in the United States; and though some doubted the reform character of this step, its supporters could point to a decline in alcohol-related diseases. In 1920, Tennessee became the pivotal state to ratify the Nineteenth Amendment, giving women the right to vote and thereby doubling the electorate. In states and localities, Progressives won other changes, including laws limiting factory hours for women and children, controlling adulteration of drugs and foods, and licensing and regulating health care practitioners.

With acute sensitivity to the political winds, President Roosevelt increasing captured the leadership of the Progressives. His solution to the trusts was to make sure that government possessed more power than they did. When he left the White House in 1909, he believed that he was handing over the reins to one of like mind. But President William Howard Taft, although he brought more antitrust actions in four years than Roosevelt had in eight, proved too conservative for Roosevelt's taste, and in 1912 he challenged Taft for renomination. The effort failed, and Roosevelt took his supporters out of the Republican fold and formed the Progressive, or Bull Moose, Party. Meanwhile, the Democrats nominated Woodrow Wilson, governor of New Jersey, the nation's most urban state. All three candidates insisted they represented the true forces of reform. Wilson won with only forty percent of the vote, but the Democrats claimed a mandate for aggressive changes. The new administration pushed through the Federal Reserve System – designed to make the currency responsive to business conditions – the Federal Trade Commission, and a separate Cabinet department for Labor.

After two decades of ferment, the reform impulse in America may have naturally run its course, but the coming of the Great War in Europe diverted the public's mind from domestic affairs to foreign policy, specifically whether or not the nation ought to intervene. Believing that war would damage democracy at home, President Wilson hoped to preserve America's neutrality. It was not to be. After three years of stalemate on the land, Germany hoped for breakthrough on the seas, and the Kaiser ordered unrestricted submarine warfare against ships of neutrals. German U-boats begin sinking American vessels without warning, and in April 1917 Congress voted overwhelming for war.

All dressed up .... A family poses around its proudest possession – a Ford car – in Albany, Minnesota, in 1917.

Wilson had asked for the declaration, but, just as he feared, the passions stirred up by war frayed the fragile fabric of trust and consensus at home. Anti-German feeling led to reprisals against innocent citizens of Teutonic heritage. Prosecutors and courts curtailed civil liberties of opponents of American involvement. America's brief involvement – from April 1917 to the Armistice eighteen months later – probably gave the Allies the victory, but at a fearful price: more than three hundred thousand casualties, forty-one billion dollars, and the smashing of the Progressive hopes for a more democratic society.

Tired and disillusioned, Americans voted Republican Warren Harding into the White House in 1920. The new symbols of the postwar age became the automobile and the radio, the faintly sinful syncopation of jazz, the flapper with her cigarette and illicit gin, the flickering screen and rinky-tink piano. The new mass circulation magazines, like Henry Luce's *Time*, depicted this self-indulgent, materialistic, consumer culture for millions of readers.

The city surged into the countryside as roads were laid to accommodate cars that mass production now made affordable to all. The census of 1920 revealed that for the first time more Americans lived in "urban places" than in "rural places." Columnists and pundits interpreted many events in the national life as the dying gasp of small-town life as metropolitan society overwhelmed it. But mere residence in a city did not confer a liberal outlook: politicians from the urban northeast sought new restrictions on immigration from southern and eastern Europe, and some new neighborhoods voted out the saloon, which served as a political and cultural center for immigrants.

Social conflicts marked the times. An agricultural depression jolted the countryside. The Ku Klux Klan worked its nativist and racist influence in politics, especially in the Midwest. In Tennessee, John Thomas Scopes was put on trial for teaching a scientific theory about the development of life on earth that according to state law and his prosecutors contradicted the plain words of the Bible. But mainly, the great gilt milky way of prosperity glittered overhead. But then the stars began to fall.

There had been signs and portents; most ignored them, and many did not grasp the implications of Black Thursday, October 29, 1929, when thirteen million shares of stock were sold on the New York Stock Exchange and prices collapsed. J. P. Morgan and John D. Rockefeller tried to stay the disaster by buying, but the old lions of America's gilded age could do nothing now.

Herbert Hoover, once admired throughout America for brilliantly organizing a relief program to postwar Europe, was President. Out of his experience in voluntarism, he urged states, localities and private localities to respond, as everywhere men were thrown out of work. Hoover believed that the federal government ought not, indeed, according to the Constitution could not, grant relief or even run a deficit to provide public jobs. Let conditions strike bottom, the President counseled, then the economy would bounce back.

Instead, industrial unemployment remained above thirty percent, with half the people out of work in some cities. Bankruptcies savaged family life as factories ground to a halt. Middle-class people who had put away savings lost everything when banks defaulted. Whole sectors of the economy simply stopped running. As mortgage bankers moved to foreclose on loans, some farmers took up shotguns and stood in the doorways of their homes.

Only the national government had the power to assemble resources that could relieve need on this scale and scope. Before that could happen, there had to be a President willing to expand federal powers beyond anything Washington had attempted since Reconstruction.

Let's try something, President Franklin Roosevelt urged the nation, after he defeated the well-meaning but hapless Hoover in the election of 1932. Like his cousin, Theodore, he had been Governor of New York; and when the Great Depression hit, he put state machinery behind aid programs for the jobless. Now such simple relief became the new administration's first priority. In time a plethora of programs, including the Works Progress Administration and the Civilian Conservation Corps, provided jobs from raking leaves to building parks, to giving musical concerts. A desultory and improvised attack on the crisis, these measures nonetheless gave the American people a sense that their government was trying to help them.

Ultimately Roosevelt's "New Deal" vastly expanded the federal role in the economic and social life of the nation. At the administration's behest Congress established a minimum wage and provided that employers must compensate workers injured on the job. Under certain conditions people out of work could qualify for unemployment insurance. And in the best known and most far-reaching program, the New Deal created the Social Security system, a tax on wages paid into a trust fund for the

Congressman Fred Hartley of New Jersey buys an apple from an unemployed man in front of the Capitol during the Depression of the Thirties.

worker's old age. For the first time blacks and other minorities could qualify for relief and benefits, formerly denied them in many states and localities.

The great middle class shared in the Roosevelt recovery strategies. A program insuring bank deposits meant that people could put their money back in the banks without fear of losing it. The government also increased the numbers of persons who could qualify to buy a home by assuring below-market interest rates on mortgages. But the New Deal was decidedly less successful in tackling the nation's persistent agricultural woes. It sought to aid the small farmer by keeping prices for his products at a level that would sustain him. The Rural Electrification Administration and the Tennessee Valley Authority enabled country people to swap their kerosene lamps for electric lights and appliances. But the movement of people off the land, first apparent in 1920, continued, and the old dream of Democrats like Thomas Jefferson, of a nation of sturdy, independent, self-sufficient yeomen receded.

The New Deal was not a coherent plan. It was based on the President's instinct for "trying something"; and it was good politics. In channeling massive amounts of public works and relief dollars to the stricken cities, the administration inadvertently aided the old enemies of Progressivism, the municipal bosses. Now the architects of the New Deal, many of whom had begun their careers as urban reformers, saw their ideas enacted by and through the machines that they had once fought. The big-city mayors were only too glad to distribute aid from Washington among the poor and unemployed, who gratefully sustained them in office. It was a classic case of "politics making strange bedfellows" – but it gave the Democrats a winning national coalition for twenty years.

The expansion of the federal government's role in the nation's life touched off tumultuous debate in the press and in Congress, especially after traditionally Republican districts in the midwest returned to their old loyalties. Republican presidential candidates accepted the New Deal, but attacked what they saw as its excesses and overweening exercise of power. Nonetheless, Roosevelt was reelected to unprecedented third and fourth terms, in 1940 and 1944.

Although historians credit the New Deal with preserving the basic capitalistic and democratic system in the worst crisis since the Civil War, Roosevelt's administrations did not restore

productivity or employment to their pre-Depression levels. Only another world war did that.

Adolf Hitler of Nazi Germany and Benito Mussolini of Fascist Italy had, through rearmament and militarization of their countries, attacked the unemployment and social unrest that came with the Depression. By the mid 1930s Japan joined with those European powers to form the Axis, an alliance that would support each member's ambitions for conquest.

Americans, by and large, wanted to believe that no country would start another war after the savagery that the Great War had unleashed across three continents. This isolationist sentiment constrained President Roosevelt, who deeply distrusted the European dictators, an attitude he shared with Winston Churchill. Their views proved justified when Hitler invaded Poland in 1939. After France fell before the Nazi onslaught the next year, many in the United States believed the nation would have to intervene to save Britain, standing alone. Still, it was not the bombs falling on London but the attack by Japan on the Pacific fleet at Pearl Harbor on December 7, 1941, that ended America's hopes for neutrality. The next day the President asked for and received from Congress a declaration of war upon Japan. Her European allies promptly declared war on the United States.

Suddenly the controversies over Washington's proper role in the national life ceased. To win the victory, the federal government had to plan, organize, marshal and allocate every resource, from armaments to foodstuffs. Americans expected and supported this national coordination of their economic life, just as they supported the war effort with virtual unanimity.

The victory of the Allies – Britain, France, the Soviet Union, and the United States – was followed by ironic consequences. The United States, which had wanted to stay out of Europe's troubles, emerged as the most militarily and economically powerful country in the world. Refusing to join the League of Nations after World War I, it now became the home (and the financial mainstay) of the United Nations. Within twenty years after they won the war, Britain and France lost their overseas empires to nationalist movements of native peoples. Over the next forty years, the defeated powers, Germany and Japan, became the most economically productive and technologically innovative nations of the world. And in perhaps the most consequential event after 1945, the United States and the Soviet Union began a "cold war," putting behind them the years of friendship and alliance that had enabled them together to prevail against Germany and Japan.

Unquestionably, Stalinist Russia exploited the victory in the west by seizing Baltic nations that had their own cultures and traditions. That would justify the United States' policy, during the administration of Harry Truman, Roosevelt's successor, of creating the North Atlantic Treaty Organization and pledging its new might to the defense of Europe and the free sectors of Berlin, in particular. As to the rest of the world, the United States adopted the policy of containment, of stopping Communism – which the State Department regarded as a monolithic force directed from Moscow – wherever it threatened.

While conceding Soviet hegemony over eastern Europe, the United States engaged communist regimes on other fronts. After Mao Tse-Tung drove America's ally, Chiang Kai-Shek, from mainland China, a wave of anti-communist hysteria gripped America. The investigations by U.S. Senator Joseph McCarthy of alleged traitors in the government found little actual subversion – but the blacklisting, smears, and innuendo that characterized "McCarthyism" ruined the lives and careers of many innocent people.

Elsewhere in Asia, the United States made fateful commitments. South Korea came under American protection at the end of the war, while a Soviet-backed regime ruled north of the 38th parallel. In June, 1950, North Korea invaded the South. United Nations forces, resisting the tide, fell back, until General Douglas MacArthur staged an amphibious landing behind enemy lines and forced the invaders to withdraw. When UN troops drove on north, to the Chinese border, China sent in two hundred thousand soldiers, cleared the northern half of the country of the foreigners, then captured the southern capital of Soeul. MacArthur claimed the Truman administration was hindering him by refusing to bomb supply depots in China. The President ordered MacArthur to cease public discussion of his views in the matter, and when he did not Truman fired him. Failing to hold its military gains, China opened peace talks and the war came to an end without a conclusive victory by either side. In the United States, frustration over the outcome contributed to the election of Dwight Eisenhower, the supreme allied commander in Europe during World War II.

From the early years of the Eisenhower administration, the United States shouldered the burden of France's war in Indo-China to reestablish its colonial possession after the departure of

defeated Japan. But nationalists under Ho Chi Minh drove out the hated Europeans. Believing that Ho was a communist first and a Vietnamese second, the United States supported division of the country. In the southern half, it put its aid and its prestige behind a non-communist but oppressive regime under Ngo Dihn Diem.

Intent upon unifying the country, nationalist forces organized as the Viet Cong and allied themselves to Ho's government in Hanoi. With the bitter question, "Who lost China?" still ringing in their ears, Cold War strategists in the administration of John F. Kennedy persuaded the President to increase American military presence and financial aid to the Diem regime. Diem was overthrown in the autumn of 1963, and a few weeks later President Kennedy was murdered as he rode in a motorcade in Dallas, Texas. The new president, Lyndon Johnson, used an attack by North Vietnamese gunboats on American ships to prod Congress into authorizing him to stop further aggression by whatever means he deemed necessary. By 1968 more than half a million American soldiers were in South Vietnam.

During the first years of the war, most Americans believed official pronouncements that it could be won with one more increment of troops or one further bombing offensive, that there was "light at the end of the tunnel." But in January 1968, at the Tet lunar new year, the communist nationals mounted an offensive that showed their capacity for continuing the war despite the brutal losses inflicted by American airpower, technological superiority, and bravery. Johnson, facing powerful challengers for renomination, announced that he would stop the bombing of the north in a bid for peace and not seek another term as president. His successor in the White House was Eisenhower's vice president, Richard Nixon. Promising, during his campaign, a secret plan to end the war, Nixon was shown after the election to have been indulging in so much rhetoric, but his administration pledged the gradual withdrawal of U.S. forces as South Vietnamese could be substituted for them. The war ground on, bitterly unpopular at home. Finally, in early 1973 the administration concluded an agreement to get its troops out on terms that could probably have been had four years earlier.

The war had been a useless, stupid mistake, the "greatest foreign policy blunder in U.S. history," said Senator Albert Gore of Tennessee. More than fifty seven thousand American soldiers died for nothing at all. In the spring of 1974 North Vietnamese troops took Saigon, the southern capital, and reunified the country. The photograph of the last American helicopter leaving the roof of the U.S. Embassy, with loyal South Vietnamese grabbing for the skids, haunted the mind.

Despite the disaster of Vietnam, the United States successfully pursued other foreign policy initiatives. For twenty-five years after the end of World War II, Germany remained a place where the next world war might start. Both the country and the capital of Berlin were divided between east and west. The NATO allies insisted on freedom of access to Berlin, deep in East Germany, while the Soviet Union built a great wall between its sector of the city and the sectors controlled by the west. In the early 1970s, however, a number of treaties and agreements fixed the borders and the status quo, thus resolving a tense, festering Cold War issue.

The capacity of the two superpowers to annihilate each other, and in that fratricide destroy the planet, increased throughout the postwar decades. The United States always achieved the newest improvement in mega-death machines first – the atomic bomb, the hydrogen bomb, the intercontinental ballistic missile – but the Soviet Union caught up within a few years. Although a 1972 treaty prevented the deployment of anti-ballistic missiles, further arms control agreements between the two nations eluded negotiators for another fifteen years. In the same period the "nuclear club" grew as small nations spent their treasuries on developing warheads and rockets to carry them to their enemies. Whether large or small, all nations in this arms race paid an enormous price for the supposed might and prestige that having the bomb imparted. No one could say for sure how much was enough superiority in a nuclear world. If one's enemy had the newest destructive capacity, didn't one's own nation have to have it, too, even though each side already possessed the firepower to obliterate the other?

The rise of the former colonies of Britain and France to places on the world stage challenged the minority non-white population of the United States to assert their rights, won in the nation's civil war but denied for a hundred years. Other sources, to be sure, gave rise to the civil rights movements, the most important social struggle in postwar America. One was the consciousness created among the black soldiers who had fought the dictators Hitler, Mussolini, and Tojo, only to return home to "Whites Only" signs in restaurants and bus terminals. Since the 1930s, the National Association for the Advancement of Colored People had, through litigation, chipped away at this edifice of laws restricting blacks in public accommodations and higher education. Then in 1954 the NAACP won a major victory when the U.S. Supreme Court ruled that the nation's dual system of public schools was inherently unequal and that desegregation must proceed "with all deliberate speed."

Black leaders were not long in challenging the other forms of racial discrimination that kept their people at the bottom of the ladder, whether the measure was health, income, or education. The genius of the civil rights movement, and one of the great Americans of the twentieth century, was Dr. Martin Luther King, Jr. Influenced by Mohandas Gandhi and his tactic of nonviolent resistance that had helped liberate India from British rule, King urged his followers to love those who hated them. He depicted the struggle as essentially moral, a fight to right an ancient moral wrong and to make the nation to live up to the words of its Declaration of Independence and Constitution that promised equal rights to all.

Dr. Martin Luther King Jr., a Baptist minister and a civil rights leader who advocated nonviolence in his campaigns against the segregation of Negroes. He won the Nobel Peace Prize in 1964.

King won millions of white allies to the struggle, and the movement effected a virtual revolution in the daily lives of Americans. Blacks and other minorities gained access to jobs, colleges, stores, hotels, restaurants, housing; all adding up to a chance for a better life. For a time, this, the American dream, flourished in the black community.

King died by an assassin's bullet in April 1968, just as those in the civil rights movement who called for cultural separation and "black power" seemed to be gaining control of the great cause. At the same time, the growing frustration over the morass in Vietnam and the economic dislocation of the war economy was causing many white people to doubt whether the nation could afford to spend more on social programs to redress the years of economic discrimination. And many people, honestly bewildered by the countercultural preferences for outlandish dress, free sexual behavior, and experimentation with drugs, turned to conservatives like the original cold warrior Richard Nixon, whom they elected president six months after King's murder.

As had happened with the Progressive movement, the great reform impulse of the 1960s perished in wartime. Helped by postwar abundance – economic production doubled from 1945-60 and doubled again from 1965-80 – the era had widened and deepened the possibilities in American life. A Catholic, John F. Kennedy, had been elected President, once thought impossible. Barriers against Jews, such as quotas in college admissions, were dropped. Children of laboring men and women had opportunities that exceeded their parents'.

In the post-Vietnam years, Americans returned to the kinds of materialistic pursuits and conservative values that they seemed wont to repossess after every war. To be sure, by 1980 the rate of divorces more than doubled over what it had been in 1965, but marriage, however short-lived, was still held as an ideal by most Americans. In practice, more and more people practiced serial monogamy, marrying, clinging to this partner, then divorcing.

In any case, most people seemed to want to turn away from the country's problems and continuing social divisions, to pursue their careers and personal well-being. The break-in at Democratic Party's national headquarters in Washington's Watergate Hotel on June 17, 1972 would complete the disillusion and estrangement of many from the times they lived in. The seven men arrested in the Democrats' offices had close ties to the reelection campaign of President Nixon, then in progress. Eventually, one of the seven, James McCord, identified John Mitchell, Nixon's campaign chief and former U.S. Attorney General, as having planned the burglary for purposes of gathering information about the Democrat's campaign plans. Then the director of the Federal Bureau of Investigation, Patrick Gray, admitted destroying evidence pertaining to the case at the direction of presidential aides. Finally, in June 1973, former White House counsel John Dean told a Congressional committee that President Nixon had approved payment of money to the burglars to buy their silence. Three weeks later the committee learned that all the conversations in the Oval Office were routinely taped.

For a year Nixon resisted efforts by Congress to obtain the recordings that would prove or disprove Dean's testimony. In July 1974 the Supreme Court ordered him to turn them over. At the same time, the House Judiciary Committee voted three articles of impeachment. Nixon's presidency was finished. The tapes disclosed that he had indeed committed an impeachable offense – a felony at law, obstruction of justice – by ordering the FBI to halt its investigation of the Watergate burglary shortly after it occurred. And here for all to hear was the gutter language, the petty politics, the obsessive vindictiveness of a man bent on destroying his political opponents by wiretaps and sabotage, all of it discussed in the house where Lincoln, the Roosevelts, and the martyred Kennedy had once done honorable service for the nation.

On August 9, 1974, Nixon took the advice of Congressional Republicans and resigned, rather than be impeached and removed. Gerald R. Ford, the Vice President and a former Republican floor leader in the House of Representatives, succeeded him.

Ford took the helm of a deeply distressed and disillusioned nation, still reeling from the murders of national leaders, the stalemate of Vietnam, and an economy distorted by the spending of more than a hundred billion dollars to save the Vietnamese from themselves. The new president, by his own admission, was not an innovator. He proposed an economic program meant to halt inflation, but it failed to achieve that. He won release of a merchant marine crew seized by Cambodia, which bolstered the confidence of a nation that had recently suffered grave military setbacks, but otherwise had little significance for American foreign policy. Nonetheless, Ford, by his genial mein and his unassailable personal integrity, brought the nation a respite from its long season of troubles. He sought election in his own right in 1976, only to be defeated by the little-known former governor of Georgia, Jimmy Carter. But President Carter recognized his predecessor's major achievement when he opened his inaugural address by thanking Ford for helping to heal the nation.

The Carter administration's major achievement was to push forward a peace process in the Middle East by bringing together the president of Egypt and the prime minister of Israel. The quarrel between Arabs and Jews over the latters' claim to a homeland in the midst of ancient Palestine had spilled the blood of generations on the sand. New fighting erupted at intervals, and Carter's initiative achieved no guarantee of permanent peace; still, he had brought the enemies to the table.

But elsewhere in the region the administration was dealt a politically fatal blow. In the winter of 1979 a revolution led by Islamic fundamentalists toppled the American-sponsored regime of the Shah of Iran and some fifty U.S. citizens were seized as hostages. Carter tried valiantly to obtain their release, first through diplomacy, then through a military rescue attempt that ended in disaster. The failure to get the hostages home seemed to confirm the judgment that pundits had unfairly decided about Carter from the beginning of his race for the White House, that he lacked enough experience to be president.

At last, in 1980, the Republican right realized its long-held dream in the defeat of Carter by a bona-fide conservative, former actor and California governor Ronald Reagan. Many of his supporters believed and hoped that he would dismantle the vestiges of the New Deal, return America to old-fashioned moral principles, and restore America's lost prestige in military might and global influence. Indeed, the Reagan administration did slash spending for social programs and poured vast new sums into high-technology weapons systems and other arms. Without going as far as some of his backers in the business community wished, he also dismantled part of the regulatory apparatus that had been put in place to clean up the nation's environment. Claiming that business would use the money to invest in new research and technological innovation, the administration cut taxes – only to see many companies use their windfall to acquire small firms in the biggest corporate consolidation since the Gilded Age.

Reagan's tax policies contributed to creating the largest peacetime deficit in American history. But few seemed to care, as the economy continued to expand. Whether people really were better off than they had been in years was debatable, but Reagan mastered the public relations potential of the presidency and convinced an overwhelming electoral majority that it was "morning in America" again.

Writer Gary Wills called Ronald Reagan the "first post-Kennedy president." To one degree or another, John F. Kennedy's successor had stood in his shadow, measured in the public mind not so much by what Kennedy had achieved but by the impossible standard of what he might have done had he not been cut down at the peak of his promise. Coming out of Hollywood, Reagan told Americans they could have all the dreams that they had denied themselves, and he urged them to get on with the business of life, which was to get and spend. The era of Kennedy ended as Reagan raised his hand to take the Presidential oath. And, it seemed, America's time of perplexity as a troubled giant ended, too. Within the hour of Reagan's becoming president, the hostages in Iran were released after more than a year in captivity.

The good life is the American dream, and the good life for most Americans most of the time means that prosperity is the main measure. But as George Bush entered the White House in 1989, many Americans were aware that while they had much, others had little or nothing. Homeless people tented on the streets of the nation's capital. One American child in five was growing up in a home with an income inadequate to provide basic necessities that could give a start in life. Given the high cost of health care, a serious illness could bankrupt almost any family. And for forty years of economic growth all Americans had paid a price in the spoiling of great portions of their beautiful country and the polluting of its air, water, and natural habitats.

Some historians see the nation's past as a cycling of periods of ferment and reform followed by periods of conservatism and consolidation. As they entered the 1990s, Americans marked the end of the Cold War abroad and, at home, awaited the next turning of the wheel.

Above: Samuel F. B. Morse. Though a gifted portrait painter, Morse is best remembered for the invention of the telegraph. His famous code of dots and dashes, transmitted over wires by electricity, bridged America's vast distances. His first message, "What hath God wrought?," traveled between Baltimore and Washington in 1844. Morse developed telegraph lines that could be laid under the ocean, linking the United States and Europe.

Top right: an 1830s engine belonging to the Boston and Worcester Railroad, which ran between Boston and Albany.

Right: an early steam locomotive. Given the formal finery of the passengers, this appears to be an special outing.

Above: Margaret Fuller, a reformer and journalist who edited *The Dial*, one of the most influential literary magazines in American history. Her chief social cause was women's rights. In 1845 she published *Woman in the Nineteenth Century*, a study of the political, social, economic and intellectual status of women.

In Promontory, Utah, on May 10, 1869, the first rail line to cross the country was completed (left), and the whole nation celebrated. The railroads made possible the nation's exploitation of its immense natural resources, thereby facilitating the industrial age which transformed America in the late nineteenth century.

TO BE SOLD & LET
BY PUBLIC AUCTION,
On MONDAY the 18th of MAY, 1829,
UNDER THE TREES.

FOR SALE,
THE THREE FOLLOWING
SLAVES,
VIZ.

HANNIBAL, about 30 Years old, an excellent House Servant, of Good Character.
WILLIAM, about 35 Years old, a Labourer.
NANCY, an excellent House Servant and Nurse.

The MEN belonging to "LEECH'S" Estate, and the WOMAN to Mrs. D. SMIT.

TO BE LET,
On the usual conditions of the Hirer finding them in Food, Clothing, and Medical

THE FOLLOWING
MALE and FEMALE
SLAVES,
OF GOOD CHARACTERS.

ROBERT BAGLEY, about 20 Years old, a good House Servant.
WILLIAM BAGLEY, about 18 Years old, a Labourer.
JOHN ARMS, about 18 Years old.
JACK ANTONIA, about 40 Years old, a Labourer.
PHILIP, an Excellent Fisherman.
HARRY, about 27 Years old, a good House Servant.
LUCY, a Young Woman of good Character, used to House Work and the Nursery.
ELIZA, an Excellent Washerwoman.
CLARA, an Excellent Washerwoman.
FANNY, about 14 Years old, House Servant.
SARAH, about 14 Years old, House Servant.

Also for Sale, at Eleven o'Clock,
Fine Rice, Gram, Paddy, Books, Muslins,
Needles, Pins, Ribbons, &c. &c.

AT ONE O'CLOCK, THAT CELEBRATED ENGLISH HORSE,
BLUCHER,

A group of nineteenth-century ex-slaves saved by Harriet Tubman, far left, a slave who fled from bondage herself and then secretly returned to the South many times to help other bondsmen escape. The enslavement of blacks began in America during the seventeenth century, particularly in the South, where cotton plantations needed laborers. By 1860 four million slaves lived in the slave states.

Right: one man stands to attention for the camera in a Confederate camp in Warrington Navy Yard, Pensacola, Florida in 1861.

Born into slavery, Frederick Douglass (below) became an advisor to President Abraham Lincoln and was the most famous black American of the nineteenth century. Before the war, he lectured in the cause of abolition and published a famous autobiography. He believed the Civil War to be a crusade to end slavery – even if Lincoln did not – and he persuaded Union commanders to train blacks as soldiers.

Slavery ended as Union armies swept through the Confederacy, but peonage did not. Right and far right: black laborers pose with a wagonload of ginned cotton in 1879.

Below: George Washington Carver, who was born a slave and yet rose to become one of the most important scientists of his time. A teacher and researcher at Tuskegee Institute for nearly half a century, he helped make that school the nation's leading black college.

Above: Indians discussing their grievances with a U.S. government official in the 1890s. The Bureau of Indian Affairs, formed in 1824, was no more successful than the army in preventing Indian wars or protecting Indian rights during the nineteenth century.

Left: President Lincoln and General George McClellan in conversation at Antietam, the site of the fiercest fighting of the Civil War. There, on September 17, 1862, 23,000 men were killed or wounded. The Battle of Antietam was a Union victory only in the sense that through it Lee's invasion of the North was repulsed.

Left: workmen pause in their labors on the first oil wells in operation in the United States at Titusville, Venange County, Pennsylvania.

Below: Alexander Graham Bell opening a telephone line between New York and Chicago. Bell, a Scotsman, changed American life utterly by his invention of a way to transmit vocal sound over wire. On March 10, 1876, his assistant Thomas A. Watson, in the next room, heard over Bell's primitive amplifier, "Mr. Watson, come here. I want you."

Right: George Eastman, left, and Thomas A. Edison. The technical brilliance of the former placed the camera in the hands of millions. During the 1870s and 1880s, Eastman pioneered a machine for coating glass plates and roll film.

By 1888 he had produced the first Kodak which, priced at $25, was still too expensive for most people, but in 1900 he put on the market a camera costing only one dollar. Edison was a genius who changed the daily lives of millions throughout the world. Among his hundreds of inventions were the electric light bulb, the phonograph and the motion picture camera.

Far right top: the first aerial photograph of Boston, 1860.

Far right bottom: the building in Rochester, New York, that was the first factory owned by the Eastman company.

Lee De Forest (above) designed and built one of the earliest vacuum tubes, an invention that made radio and television communication possible over long distances. In 1910 De Forest staged the first radio musical broadcast in history from the Metropolitan Opera House in New York City.

Left: Main Street East in Nantucket, Massachusetts, in 1897 – as yet, not a car in sight.

Personifying the American vision of the self-made man, Henry Ford (left) demonstrated mechanical proficiency even as a child. While working as an engineer during the 1880s he began experiments with gasoline-powered motors. In 1899 he formed the Detroit Automobile Company, and in 1908 he brought out the Model T, sometimes called "the greatest single vehicle in the history of world transportation."

Ford pioneered two changes in manufacturing that revolutionized industry everywhere: standardized, interchangable parts and the assembly line (far left and above).

By 1916 two thousand automobiles a day were rolling out of the Ford Motor Company (above left). Economies of scale made the cost of the vehicle affordable to middle-class families everywhere.

Experts said it couldn't be done – but two self-educated bicycle mechanics from Ohio did it: Orville and Wilbur Wright built the first successful heavier-than-air flying machine. After analyzing the failures of other aviation experiments, they began to try out wing designs using kites, gliders, and wing prototypes in a wind tunnel of their own devising. On the windy dunes of Kitty Hawk, North Carolina, they put their designs to the test. On December 17, 1903, with Orville at the controls, man flew for the first time (left). Thus the brothers joined the great pantheon of this age of innovation – Carver, Bell, Eastman, Edison, De Forest and Ford, who made it seem as if anything man could dream, he could do.

Above: Wilbur Wright sits at the controls of one of the early airplanes in 1908.

Women attempt to sew piecework by the light of a naked gas flame connected to the stove in their kitchen. Although apparently bright in this photograph – the flash for the camera gives the illusion of a well-lit room – this light would not have been sufficient to properly illuminate their work. This, the thin drape at the bedroom window, the hanging shawl that would have to serve as a coat and the bare floor suggest considerable poverty. Nevertheless, the possession of a sewing machine gave a woman the chance to make money, albeit very little, as a pieceworker.

The evergreens of Washington State tower over a steam engine in 1895; yet lumbermen were already felling the great trees by tens of thousands and hauling them away for fuel. The great industrial expansion of the late 1800s ran on coal, timber and oil. By the dawn of the new century, the need for the conservation of America's natural resources was clear. In the West, President Theodore Roosevelt created a forest preserve of fifteen million acres and set aside from sale eighty-five million acres in Alaska. His concern for wild areas earned him an enduring place in the memory of Americans who love the land.

Trappers stand beside one hundred thousand dollars worth of furs on the wharf at Nome, Alaska, in August, 1906. Eight years before, Nome had become universally popular when gold was discovered, bringing thousands north to the creeks and beaches of this region.

Above: with fife and drum, these troops might be ushering Uncle Sam onto the stage as a world power. The Spanish-American War, from April to August, 1898, took place over Cuba. The powerful journalist William Randolph Hearst told the readers of his newspapers that Spanish misrule of the island had caused the death of a quarter of its population. Although this report was exaggerated, many Americans believed that the U.S. should intervene. In the course of the ensuing war, the United States acquired Guam, Puerto Rico and the Philippines.

Crowds cheered and kept time to the martial and patriotic music of John Philip Sousa (right) which captured the spirit of the exuberant age. "The Stars and Stripes Forever" would long be heard at high school commencements, the parades of returning veterans and Presidential inaugurations.

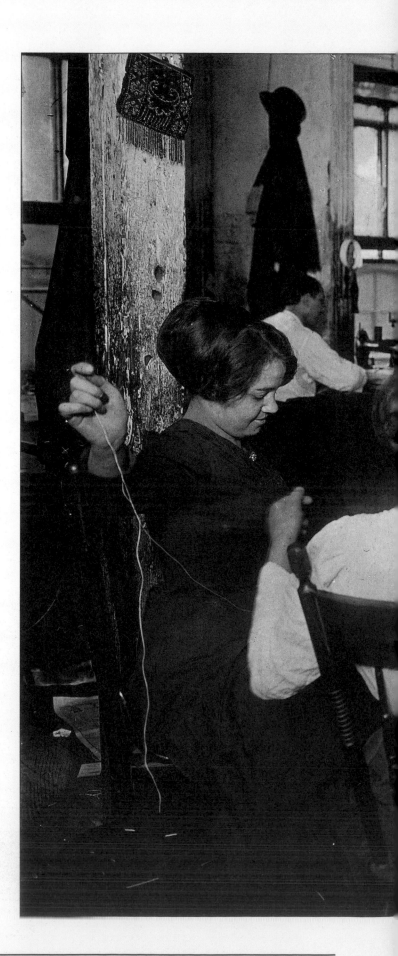

A nurse who had tended the wounded in the Civil War, Clara Barton (above) founded the American Red Cross and placed it at the service of civilians in times of disaster. For all the greed and striving of the era, many Americans sought to make the life of the nation fairer, more democratic and more gentle. Some were political, like the Populists and the Progressives. Others worked anonymously in slums, settlement houses and patriotic organizations.

By the early twentieth century, a new social conscience was stirring reformers concerned about working conditions in factories. This small garment mill in a loft (right) was relatively humane – at least there were windows – compared to many workplaces.

A sewing room, one of many crowded into
New York City's famous garment district.
Garment workers founded the Knights of Labor
shortly after the Civil War. This union utilized
strikes, boycotts and bargaining, and by 1886
had grown to some seven hundred
thousand members.

Wooden floors and furniture were typical of a small office (right) prior to the First War.

Below: a female typing pool of some sixty or more women typical of large offices in 1907. A certain "respectable" uniformity of dress would have been expected of a woman office worker – note that all hair was worn long, but pinned up, all collars buttoned to the throat, all blouses styled with leg of mutton sleeves.

Above: refugees from the devastating 1906 San
Francisco earthquake retain a few possessions
and a certain dignity as they sit down to lunch
on Franklin Street, near Fulton Street, after
the disaster.

Right: on a sunlit Second Avenue, garment
workers parade in strength in New York
in 1910.

The aftermath of the 1906 San Francisco earthquake in Sansome and California streets, where firemen pose in front of the shattered facade of Halsey Bank. In reality, it was the fires following the earthquake that did the most damage to the city. After the inferno had raged for three days and nights, three-quarters of San Francisco's homes, businesses and hotels had been destroyed.

Hands on hips, a convict pauses in his drudgery on a Florida farm in 1910 to throw a baleful stare at the photographer. Until the nineteenth century, convict labor was used chiefly as an added punishment and was often unproductive. Later, outdoor public works, such as farming, road building and reforestation, used convict labor to considerable effect. The use of the notorious chain gangs of some Southern states, in which convicts were chained and forced to do heavy labor, has declined but not disappeared today.

Left: members of the Women's Auxiliary Typographical Union celebrate Labor Day in 1909 in New York City.

Right: a poster produced by a group of anti-suffrage women.

Below: Elizabeth Cady Stanton, standing, and Susan B. Anthony. In 1848, these women organized the first women's suffrage convention in Senaca Falls, New York.

Mr. Voter:

VOTE NO

ON WOMAN SUFFRAGE

NOVEMBER 6

The Ballot will secure a Woman no Right that she Needs and does not Possess

WOMAN'S ANTI SUFFRAGE ASSOCIATION
280 MADISON AVENUE
NEW YORK

The headquarters of Women Voters in Cleveland in 1912. To prevail, the suffragists had to convince men to let them have the right of the ballot. After all, only men could vote to give the vote to everyone!

Suffragists in New York City's Greenwich Village in 1912 haul up a banner to express their frustration. By 1919 all nineteen states west of the Mississippi allowed a woman to vote. Five limited her to Presidential elections, but the rest permitted her to vote in every contest. If women in the West could cast the vote, why couldn't women everywhere?

Congress had to approve the "Anthony Amendment," guaranteeing women the right to vote, before it could be submitted to the states for ratification. Standing on the south lawn of the United States Capitol in 1913, suffragists (above) smiled as they tried persuasion. Others picketed the White House, were arrested, stripped and thrown into jail.

In 1919 Congress passed the amendment that would enfranchise women, and distributed it to the states. Right: the Speaker of the House of Representatives signing the legislation.

"The right of citizens of the United States to vote shall not be denied or abridged by the United States or any state on account of sex." Three-fourths of the forty-eight states had to ratify this amendment for it to become part of the Constitution. Facing page: Alice Paul unfurls a banner decorated with a star for every state that voted for ratification at the headquarters of the National Women's Party.

Above: Carrie Chapman Catt, president of the National American Woman Suffrage Association, receives a bouquet from Governor Smith of New York in 1920.

Right: women register to vote in the primaries in New York City in September, 1920.

Facing page left: the flagbearer in a suffrage parade, circa 1910.

Facing page right: Margaret Sanger with her sister in a courtroom in 1916. A committed feminist, Sanger founded the Planned Parenthood Federation of America. In advertizing contraception, she broke the law, hence her appearance in court.

Right: women pacifists working against the nation's entry into the Great War. *The New York Call*, which they are distributing, urges ships to avoid the war zone. Yet Germany's attacks on merchant vessels would lead President Wilson to ask Congress for a declaration of war.

The Woman's Christian Temperance Union (below) promoted abstinence from intoxicating drink. The W.C.T.U. became a powerful force in the movement that saw the passage of the Eighteenth Amendment in 1919, prohibiting the manufacture, sale, import, and export of alcohol in the United States.

Above: a detail of American Negro troops of
the First World War engaged in building a
railway line from Brest to the front line in
October, 1918.

Above: a woman running a factory lathe during
the First World War – a job done by a man
before the war and one which would be done
by a man again once the war was won.

Nearly a fifth of the war-time American work
force was made up of women, who assumed
new responsibilities in industry as men left for
the front. Right: an automotive mechanics class
for women in 1917.

Above and above right: Charlie Chaplin as the wistful little tramp in the Hollywood film *Gold Rush* in 1924. By the mid-Twenties Chaplin was producing films, starring in them and even writing their background music.

Right: a scene from *Easy Street*, 1917, in which Chaplin plays a well-meaning but ineffectual policeman.

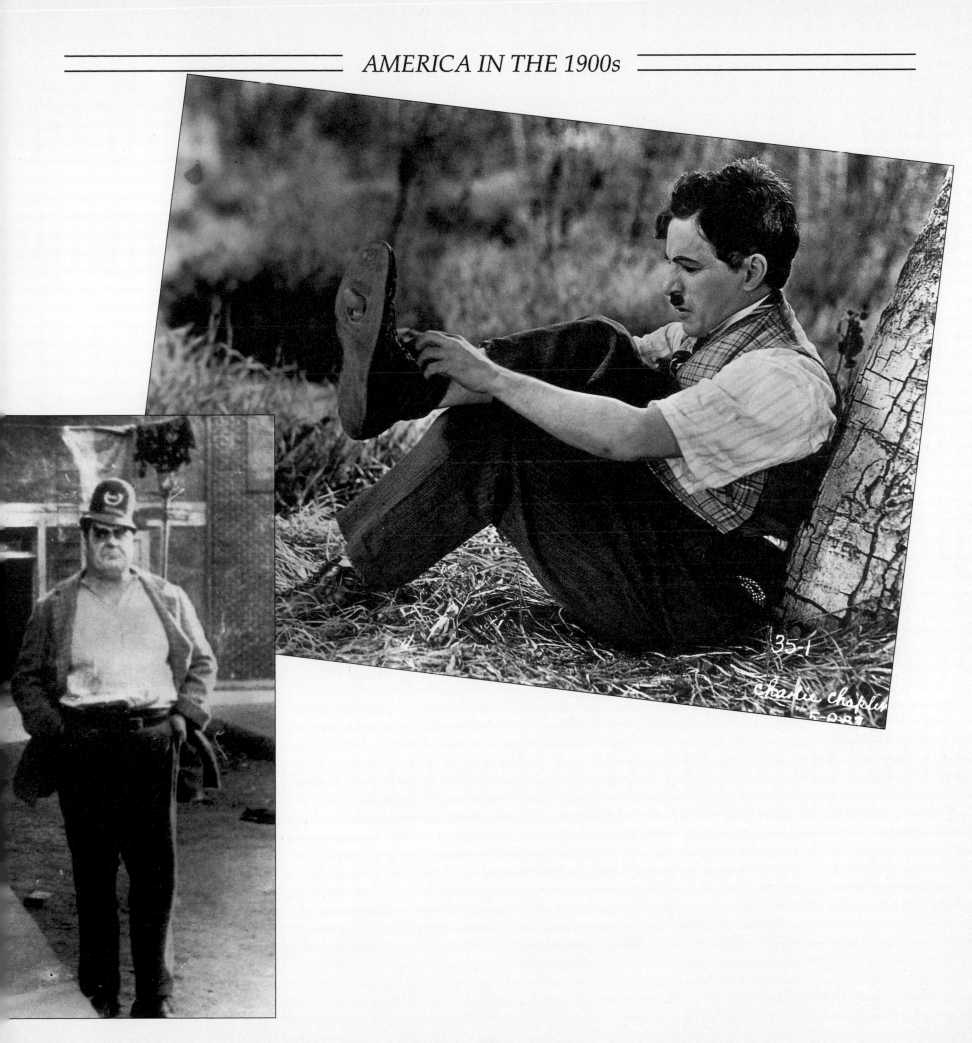

The United States financed its participation in the war through the sales of Liberty Bonds. Left: Charlie Chaplin urges the crowd to come forward and buy them at a rally in April, 1918.

Below: Chaplin in *Gold Rush*, one of his most successful films.

Black troops from the 369th Infantry are welcomed home with a chicken dinner upon returning from Europe after the end of the First World War. Germany signed the armistice treaty at 5.00am on November 11, 1918. Six hours later the guns fell silent, and one of the greatest calamities in human history was over.

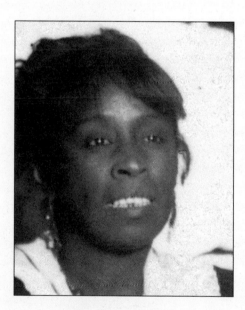

Despite the coming of peace, passions did not cool. In 1919 U.S. Attorney General Mitchell A. Palmer ordered raids without warrants on labor organizations and private homes, targeting what he alleged was a Bolshevik uprising. In one night the Justice Department arrested four thousand immigrants (left). Three hundred innocent citizens of Detroit were detained for a week. The plot proved to be wholly of Palmer's imagining.

Above: children from a devastated Europe view
the New York skyline from Ellis Island in 1919.
An immigration officer is introducing them to
their new country.

Emma Goldman addresses a crowd in New York City's Union Square in 1916. Palmer succeeded in deporting some Americans of foreign birth, including Emma Goldman, who had long been an outspoken proponent of labor radicalism, birth control, and women's rights. She went to prison for two years for opposing the draft during the Great War and later Palmer sent her to her native Russia. Goldman returned to the United States in 1934.

In another manifestation of the "Red Scare," Nicola Sacco and Bartolomeo Vanzetti (left and far left respectively) were arrested on charges of robbery and murder of the paymaster at a Massachusetts shoe factory. The state's case relied upon popular prejudices of the hour against Americans of foreign extraction, and the judge reportedly denounced the defendants after the case came before him. The trial claimed the attention of the nation. The two men were convicted in 1921 and held in jail for six years before being executed.

William Haywood (below) led the International Workers of the World, which sought to achieve socialism through unions. He was sentenced to twenty years in prison for his active opposition to the war. He did not serve the time, but fled the country instead.

Some workers sought to improve industrial conditions through peaceful protest. Working hours were up to fourteen hours a day, seven days a week. These women union members are picketing a Republican convention in New York City, seeking a six-day working week of eight hours a day.

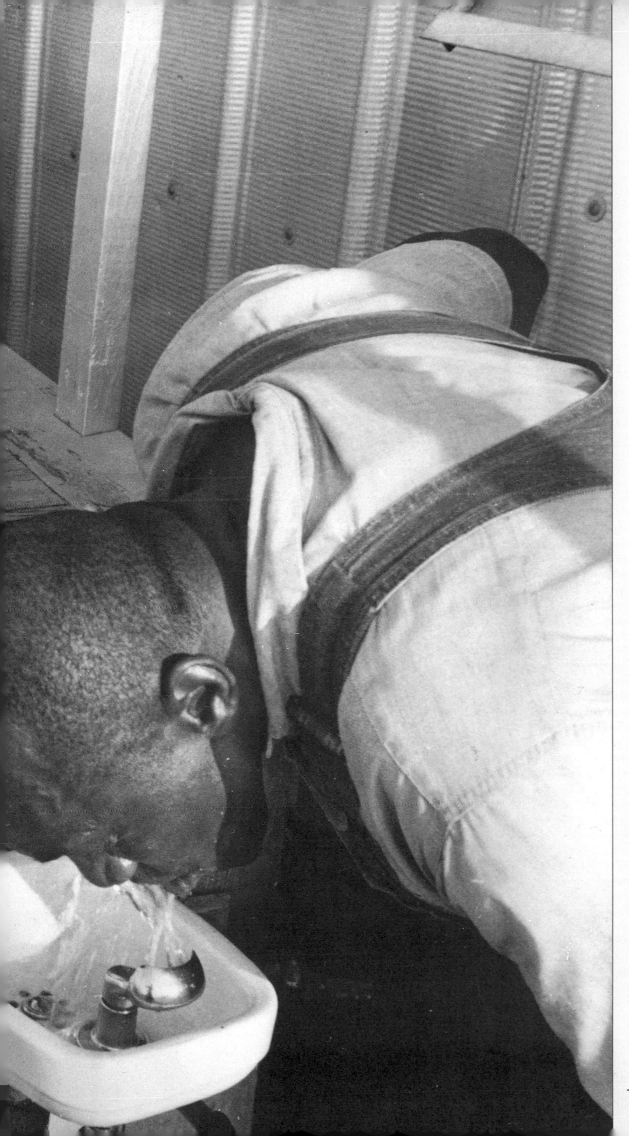

During the years after the Civil War, black people and white people in the South had lived on the same streets, attended the same churches and gone to the polls at election time. Beginning around 1890, a series of harsh, repressive laws passed by state legislatures and city councils separated the races. By 1920 apartheid applied even at drinking fountains.

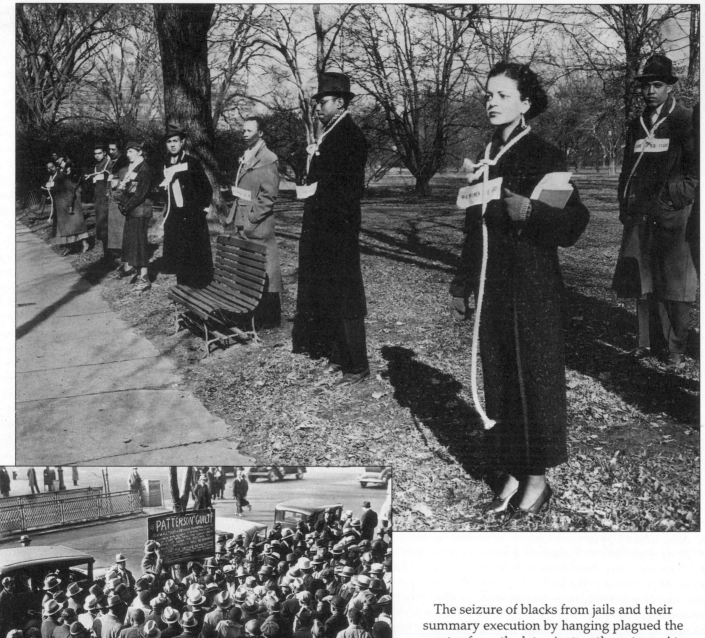

The seizure of blacks from jails and their summary execution by hanging plagued the country from the late nineteenth century. At a 1934 protest in Washington, D.C., demonstrators (above) wore lengths of rope around their necks to make their point.

When a jury in Alabama convicted nine young black men of raping two white women in 1932, despite countervailing evidence, a Harlem gathering (left) denounced the verdict.

New York's Harlem precinct rioted in 1943. Five people died and five million dollars in property damage ensued. Black proprietors hastily hung handmade signs (right) to identify their "colored stores."

These black sharecropper families were evicted from plantations in southeast Missouri during the Great Depression.

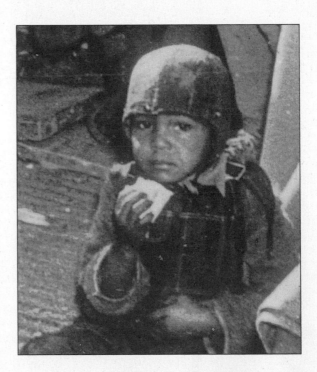

Below: Knights of the Ku Klux Klan saluting the American flag and the firey cross in the Twenties, when the Klan's membership was at its peak and numbered between four and five million. The power of this much feared organization declined in the Thirties after the passing of state laws that forbade the wearing of masks and thereby eliminated the secret element.

Below: the speaker's stand at a Klansmen's rally on Long Island. The Klan stood for white supremacy, and was often anti-semitic, anti-homosexual and anti-Catholic. It was responsible for lynchings and whippings, methods it adopted when intimidation proved an inadequate means of achieving its aims.

Left: a 1986 meeting of Klansmen at East Windsor, Connecticut.

The Wall Street Crash of 1929. When the market crashed, millions of people who couldn't get to the bank in time lost their life savings. The Great Depression began with lines of confused depositers locked out of their banks. Once the initial shock of the crash was over, Wall Street itself became comparatively deserted.

Out of work, veterans of the Great War appealed to Congress to pay the bonus awarded them for their service, which offered twenty year annuities, immediately. Marching toward Washington in 1931, veterans (left) encamped at Johnstown, Pennsylvania.

Some 17,000 men, "the Bonus Army," set up their tents in Washington. When a bill that would have paid veterans for their bonus certificates was defeated, most left, but some two thousand stayed. In July, 1932, President Hoover sent in troops to evict them (below).

Right: a U. S. congressman buys an apple from an unemployed man.

Below: a member of the ragged "hunger army" that marched on the New Jersey state capitol in the spring of 1936 seeking relief. The volume in his grasp evidently lulled him to sleep.

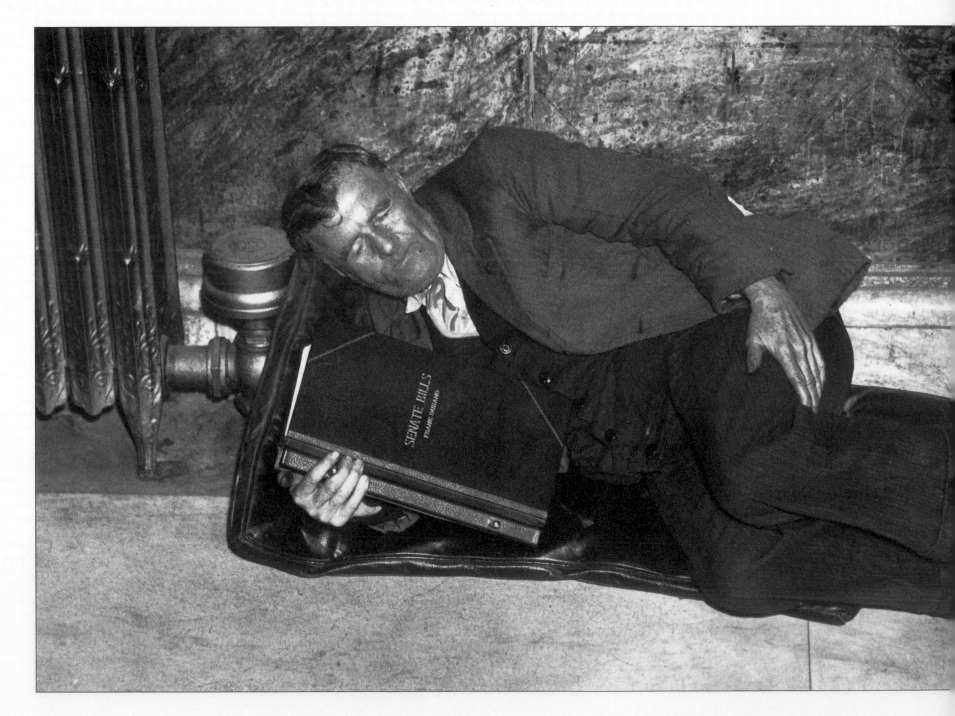

The Great Depression struck middle-class families as well as those already living on the economic margins of society. Left: a couple and their children who have been turned out of their house in La Grange, Georgia.

Below: Public Safety Director "Duckboard" Butler smashing kegs of beer and pouring them into the Schuylkill River, Philadelphia, in 1924, as part of the government's attempts to impose Prohibition.

President Franklin D. Roosevelt created the National Recovery Administration in 1933. The N.R.A. was one of many "alphabet soup" agencies that the administration set up in an effort to lift the nation out of its economic plight. Business and industries cooperating with N.R.A. codes of fair competition displayed its symbol, a blue eagle. Left: children in San Francisco forming a blue eagle.

Below: F.D.R. visits a Civilian Conservation Corps camp in the Thirties and is heartily cheered by men he helped put to work.

On December 30, 1936, the United Auto Workers struck at the General Motors Plant in Flint, Michigan. They occupied the plant by sitting down and ignoring management's orders to leave. Outside, their wives formed a "women's auxiliary" and picketed in support of the sit-in. Among the workers' other demands was one that would make the U.A.W. their sole bargaining agent. After forty-three days, these happy strikers got to go home.

The days of boom and bust had their heroes. Louis Armstrong, a New Orleans-born Negro, became an internationally famous jazz soloist. Here he rehearses on the trumpet, his mastery of which made him famous. His improvisational style on jazz themes greatly influenced that musical genre.

Charles A. Lindbergh (left) became the most celebrated person in the world when he made the first airplane flight from New York to Paris. Flying alone in a fragile little craft of his own design – *The Spirit of St. Louis* – Lindbergh completed the journey in thirty-three-and-a-half hours on May 20-21, 1927. Never comfortable in the spotlight, nonetheless the aviator lived out most of his life in its glare.

Amelia Earhart (facing page) became the first woman to fly across the Atlantic, an achievement which she accomplished with two men. In 1932 she made the journey solo and in record-breaking time, taking only thirteen-and-a-half hours from Newfoundland to Ireland. Further records followed, as did public adulation. In 1937 she and her navigator embarked on a round-the- world flight, only to disappear over the Pacific Ocean. No trace of her or the aircraft was ever found.

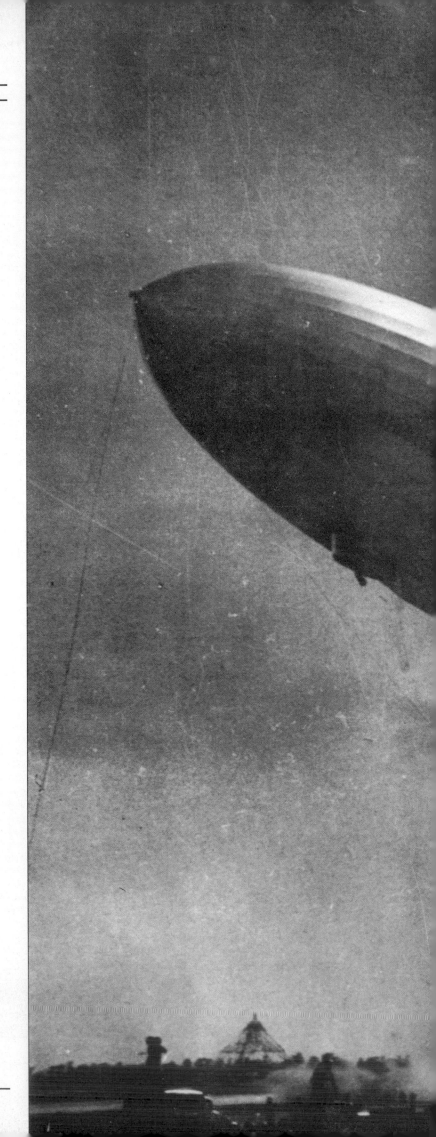

The giant German Zeppelin *Hindenburg* crashes
to earth in flames following an explosion on
board that occurred as it was about to be
moored to its mast at Lakehurst, New Jersey, on
May 6, 1937. Inflated with highly inflammable
hydrogen, the airship was completely
destroyed, with the loss of thirty-six lives.
Miraculously, there were sixty-one survivors.

Above: Dwight Eisenhower, who was chief of operations in Washington D.C. at the outbreak of the Second World War and a five-star general commanding the Allied forces in Germany at its close.

Left: *West Virginia*, one of the battleships destroyed in the Japanese aerial bombardment of Pearl Harbor in December, 1941.

Far left: General Douglas MacArthur. After the Japanese attack on Pearl Harbor, MacArthur commanded the defense of the Philippines until March, 1942, after which he took command of all Allied forces in the Southwest Pacific until the Japanese were defeated in 1945.

The Lend-Lease Act, passed by Congress in 1941, gave the President the power to transfer weapons, equipment, and food to any nation fighting the Axis powers. Under the measure, F.D.R. sent billions of dollars in supplies to Great Britain, France, and Russia. These grim-faced members of the "Mothers Crusade," kneeling in prayer near the U. S. Capitol, correctly foresaw that the United States was taking one more step towards total involvement inWorld War II.

Women took over the factory jobs as men went off to fight in the Second World War. Left: builders of B-24 "Liberator" bombers pause for lunch at the world's longest airplane assembly line in Fort Worth, Texas.

After months of secret research by its atomic scientists, the United States tested the first nuclear weapon in the New Mexico desert on July 16, 1945. Below: some of the bomb's developers examining seared sand particles at the test site. On August 6 the U. S. Air Force dropped one of the H-bombs on Hiroshima, Japan, with horrifying effects. Three days later a second bomb partially destroyed Nagasaki and led to the surrender of Japan.

The economy boomed after the peace, giving rise to the consumer culture, the tract house, television, and the transistor radio. In May, 1948, General Motors employees (facing page) celebrated the eleven-cent-an-hour increase that their strike had won. Having held back demands because of the war, American workers now wanted their share of prosperity.

In the years after the war, many Americans believed that the Soviets intended to subvert and conquer other nations. Fear of supposed Soviet infiltration led to U.S. Senator Joseph McCarthy's national crusade against Communism. The government also won convictions against leaders of the small, unimportant American Communist Party. At a 1949 news conference, party board member Elizabeth Gurley Flynn (above) accused the Truman administration of suppressing the party "because it represents a large segment of the population which is for peace" with the Soviet Union.

When Albert Einstein (right) fled Hitler's Germany to the United States, he was already recognized as one of the world's greatest scientists. His theory of relativity showed that matter and energy could be exchangable andthereby laid the basis for splitting the atom. A letter he wrote to President Roosevelt in 1939, warning that Germany could develop an atomic bomb, started the United States on the road that led to the production of the weapon.

Above: American mathematician John von Neumann, right, and J. Robert Oppenheimer, the physicist who directed the laboratory where the atomic bomb was built. Von Neumann developed a way to store programs in the memory of a computer, and by 1951 mass production of the machines was underway. Improvements in design, speed, and reliability followed rapidly.

Mechanization was changing the nature of work, from farm to factory floor. Farm prices achieved record highs in the postwar years, with farmers receiving more for their goods than at any time since 1920. Left: combines harvesting wheat in the Texas panhandle.

Facing page: Babe Ruth at bat. Considered the greatest of all baseball players, George Herman Ruth hit 714 home runs in major league play, a record that stood until 1974. Off the field he made headlines by visiting sick children in hospital, and a year before he died in 1948 he established and endowed the Babe Ruth Foundation to aid underprivileged youths. He was renowned almost as much for his pleasant personality as his talented and colorful play.

Left: ten-year-old Mimi Jordan drinks milk as she whirls her hula hoop for what was believed to be a record three hours in 1958.

Above: Charlie "Bird" Parker warms up on the saxophone at the Paris Jazz Festival in 1949. One of the most influential musicians in the history of jazz, Parker dominated the 1940s jazz scene.

Right: one high school pupil attacks another in 1958 as a result of tensions over the enforced integration of schools in Little Rock, Arkansas.

In a landmark case, decided in May, 1954, the United States Supreme Court held that the legal doctrine permitting "separate but equal" public schools for black and white children violated their constitutional guarantee of equal protection under the law. The nine justices held unanimously that desegregation of the public schools must be accomplished "with all deliberate speed." Mrs. Nettie Hunt explains the court action to her daughter, Nikie, on the steps of the Supreme Court Building.

The ruling desegregating schools excited bitter opposition in parts of the South. In September, 1957, the Arkansas state militia blocked black students from entering Little Rock's Central High School. President Eisenhower ordered United States Army troops to escort nine black youngsters (left) to their classrooms.

Below: white teenagers protest against the integration of Little Rock's schools.

In the summer of 1961 civil rights activists boarded public buses and rode through the South to challenge racially separate waiting rooms and other segregation policies practiced by the carriers. This bus was attacked by an anti-civil rights mob outside Anniston, Alabama, and left to burn on the highway.

Above: Senator John F. Kennedy, left, takes the floor in a televised debate with his Republican rival, Richard Nixon, in the campaign for the Presidency in 1960. At forty-three, Kennedy was shortly to become America's youngest President.

Right: President Kennedy with his wife Jacqueline, in Dallas, Texas, on November 22, 1963. They are seated in the open car in which he was later assassinated (above right).

Far right: draped in the flag, Kennedy's coffin lies in state in the Capitol, prior to its burial in Arlington National Cemetery.

The Reverend Martin Luther King, Junior and more than three thousand followers set out on a march from Selma to Montgomery, Alabama, in the spring of 1965 to protest against voting rights discrimination. The first attempt was stopped when two hundred state troopers attacked the demonstrators. It required a federal court order and the protection of twenty-two hundred troops before the march could proceed.

Young Freddie Lee Bennett received a clubbing in the first attempt of civil rights protesters to march from Selma to Montgomery in 1965. His button reads, "We Shall Overcome," a slogan and anthem of the civil rights movement, which was dedicated to non-violence.

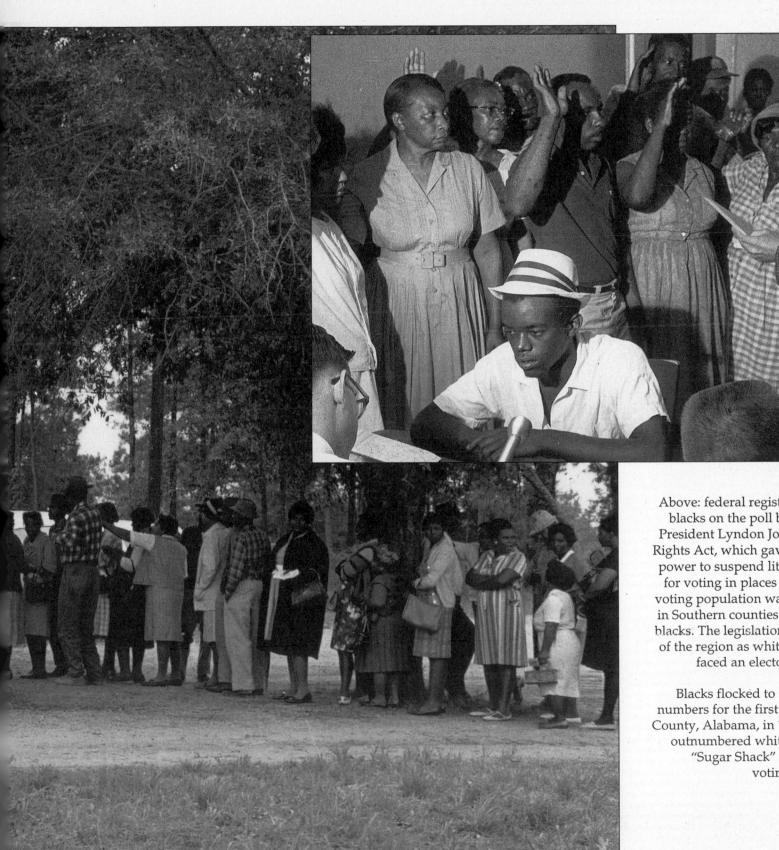

Above: federal registrars in Mississippi enrol blacks on the poll books. In August, 1966, President Lyndon Johnson signed the Voting Rights Act, which gave the federal government power to suspend literacy and character tests for voting in places where less than half the voting population was registered – in practice, in Southern counties having large numbers of blacks. The legislation transformed the politics of the region as white officeholders suddenly faced an electorate of both races.

Blacks flocked to the polls (left) in large numbers for the first time in history in Wilcox County, Alabama, in 1966. In this county blacks outnumbered whites by three to one. The "Sugar Shack" was typical of rural voting places.

Some 600 Negroes joined the Mississippi freedom marchers at a voter registration rally in Grenada, Mississippi, in June, 1966, which took place around a statue dedicated to the memory of Confederate soldiers.

Standing amid the rubble of westside Detroit, Michigan, a National Guardsman takes a watermelon break. On July 23, 1967, rioting erupted in this city following a police raid on an after-hours drinking club in a black neighborhood. The riot continued for a week, and left forty-one people dead and two thousand injured. Four hundred million dollars worth of damage was done to property and five thousand people were left without homes. This and other urban riots marked a new phase in the civil rights movement, as militants claimed nonviolent protest did too little, too slowly, to change the conditions of blacks in America.

Left: thousands of women stream up New York's Fifth Avenue on August 26, 1971, the 51st anniversary of woman's suffrage. Among their demands are "51% of everything."

The National Organization for Women presented a "Bill of Rights for Women" to political parties and candidates in the 1968 elections, intending to achieve "full equality for women, in truly equal partnership with men." Below: Dr. Kathryn F. Clarebach, left, chairman of N.O.W.'s board, and author Betty Friedan, the group's president.

However long the ideals of women's liberation might be in gaining acceptance, new work opportunities were opening for women. In 1974 a woman did a job that would probably have been denied "the weaker sex" a few years before – washing the windows (above) of San Francisco skyscrapers.

Left: Linda Sabo, mother of six and grandmother of two, shovels coal in a mine near St. Clairsville, Ohio, in 1981.

Above: demonstrators rally in front of the
Lincoln Memorial in 1981 for passage of the
Equal Rights Amendment. This proposed
changes in the Constitution that would prohibit
the denial of rights on the grounds of sex.
Although Congress extended the deadline by
which states might ratify the amendment, the
necessary two thirds failed to do so.

Facing page: Canadian women mark
International Women's Day on March 8, 1979.
Burning a bra, they protested against rape, for
abortion on demand, and in favor of equal pay
for equal work.

Bayonets fixed, National Guardsmen block Beale Street, a center of black culture and entertainment in Memphis, Tennessee, as civil rights marchers pass silently by on March 29, 1968. Six days later, Martin Luther King was shot and killed by an assassin on a Memphis motel balcony.

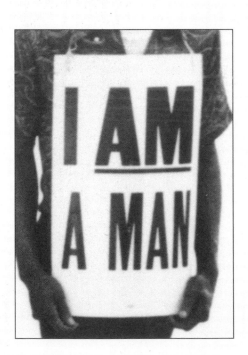

The 1960s and 1970s would see humankind venture beyond the planet. On February 20, 1962, John Glenn (right) became the first American to orbit the earth – Soviet cosmonauts and U.S. astronaut Alan Shepard had preceded him into space. In 1974 Glenn was elected a United States Senator for Ohio.

Facing page: the pilot of the Gemini 12 space vehicle, Edwin "Buzz" Aldrin, works outside the craft high over the earth in 1966. Three years later, Aldrin accompanied Neil Armstrong in the Apollo 11 landing module that landed on the moon's Sea of Tranquillity, while their fellow pilot, Michael Collins, waited overhead. The visitors left behind a plaque that read, "Here men from the planet Earth first set foot upon the moon July, 1969, AD. We came in peace for all mankind."

Below: the emblem of the Apollo 11 astronauts.

Above and left: Neil Armstrong, the first man to walk on the moon, during the Apollo 11 mission on July 21, 1969.

"One small step for man, but one giant leap for mankind," Armstrong proclaimed as he climbed down the ladder from the space module (facing page) and placed a foot on the arid surface of the Sea of Tranquillity.

Left: Dr. Robert Jarvik of the University of Utah shows the polyurethane and dacron mesh artificial heart he designed for transplanting in humans. Surgeons developed techniques for transplanting real hearts from human donors into patients dying from coronary illness, but the artificial heart eluded perfection.

Facing page: *Columbia* leaves Cape Canaveral in November, 1983, with a space laboratory in the hold. The United States focused its space program on the space shuttle during the 1980s. As its name implied, the shuttle could carry payloads into orbit in cargo bays. Its airplane-like design enabled it to return to earth and be sent aloft again with powerful booster rockets.

When in February, 1972, President Richard Nixon visited the Peoples Republic of China, he was the first President to do so since 1948 when the country was taken over by Communists. The President found time to be introduced to some Chinese children (left) whilst he was visiting Hangzhou.

He met the Chinese Prime Minister Chou En-lai (facing page) at a banquet held in his honor in Shanghai.

Above: Richard Nixon salutes the crowd prior
to leaving the White House in September, 1974,
after his resignation from the Presidency. He
was the first President in American history to
resign, a step he was obliged to take after the
corruption of his administration was exposed.

Mount St. Helens (right) in Washington state
erupted on July 22, 1980, emitting a plume of
ash and steam that rose 60,000 feet in the air.

Far left: President Carter, center, signs the historic Middle East peace treaty between Israel and Egypt in March, 1979, flanked the Egyptian President Anwar Sadat, right, and the Israeli Prime Minister Menachem Begin.

Above: four Presidents stand on the same platform in 1981 after the assassination of Anwar Sadat. From left to right: Gerald Ford, Richard Nixon, Ronald Reagan and Jimmy Carter.

Left: Sandra Day O'Connor, who became the first woman Supreme Court Justice in August, 1981.

Throughout its history, many people have
come to the United States from all over the
world to seek opportunity. These laborers from
Mexico have crossed the border into California
illegally to work in the 1980 fruit harvest and
have been rounded up by the U.S.
Border Patrol.

Nearly ten thousand people, most of them Hispanics, participate in the largest naturalization event in American history at Miami's Orange Bowl stadium in 1984. Many immigrants of Hispanic heritage became citizens, and, as the new century approached, the nation felt the influence of their numbers and their cultures in local and regional concerns.

"Keep hope alive." Jesse Jackson made the
phrase his theme in his campaign for the
Democratic Presidential nomination in 1988.
Above: Jackson and veterans of the civil rights'
struggle re-enact the march to Montgomery on
the twenty-fifth anniversary of Martin Luther
King's famous march

Right: Detroiters accepting the surplus food
that the federal government made available to
soup kitchens in 1982 after Detroit mayor
Coleman Young warned that some of his fellow
citizens would starve to death before winter
was over.

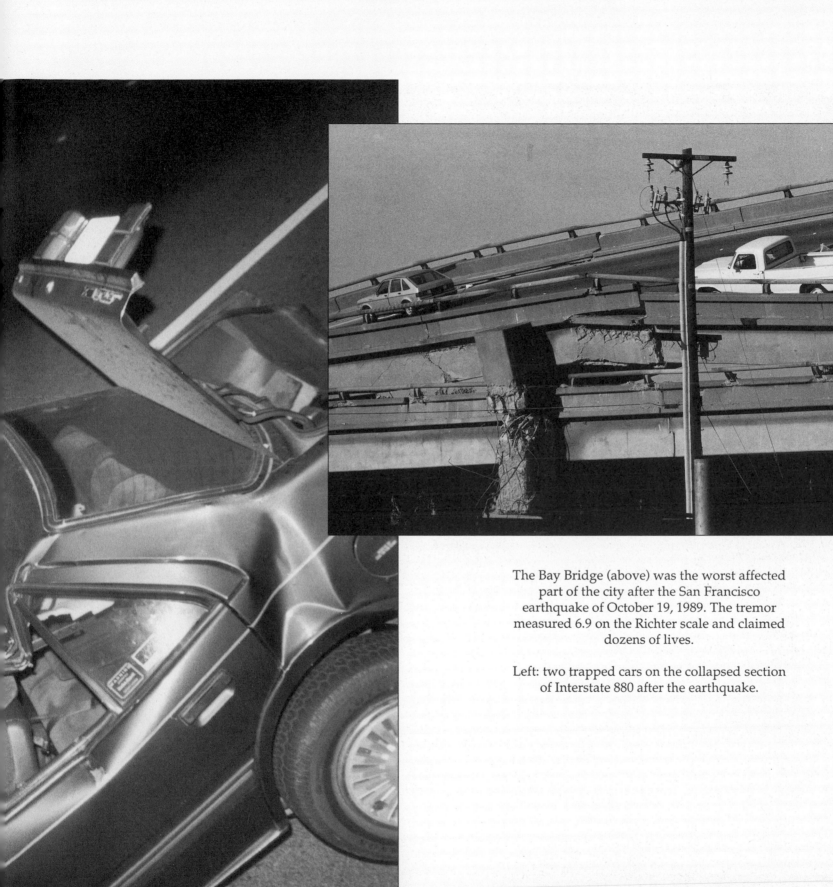

The Bay Bridge (above) was the worst affected part of the city after the San Francisco earthquake of October 19, 1989. The tremor measured 6.9 on the Richter scale and claimed dozens of lives.

Left: two trapped cars on the collapsed section of Interstate 880 after the earthquake.

Below: President Reagan and Soviet General Secretary Gorbachev on cordial terms at the Washington Summit of December, 1987. During this summit, the two world leaders signed a treaty to eliminate intermediate nuclear forces in Europe.

Right: President Elect Bush, left, President Reagan and Soviet leader Gorbachev view the skyline of New York after their meeting there in December, 1988. An earthquake in Armenia led Mr. Gorbachev to cut short his visit.

Left: the B-2 Stealth bomber pictured on a flight across California on July 18, 1989. One of the highest flying aircraft in the world, this bomber is invisible to radar.

Far left: the corpses of sea otters accumulate on the beach at Green Island after a major oil spill from the *Exxon Valdez* spreads across Prince William Sound, Alaska, in March, 1989.